The Night Rainbow

by Barbara Juster Esbensen

illustrated by Helen K. Davie

ORCHARD BOOKS　NEW YORK

FROM THE AUTHOR

MANY PEOPLE in North America
live too far south to be able to see the
aurora borealis, also known as the northern
lights. The lights of northern cities brighten
the night sky so that the aurora isn't visible
even to the people who live in or near
those cities.

I hope that my words will do three things.
First, I want them to conjure up these
heart-stopping light displays for everyone
who has never seen them.

Second, I have set down, as poetry, some
of the ancient legends from people who, for
centuries, have lived in the northern reaches
of our planet. They stared in wonderment at
the astonishing formations of light moving in
the skies above them. They imagined stories
to go with the images they thought they
could see there.

And the third reason I have written this
book: I hope that if you have ever been lucky
enough to stand in wonder yourself, under
those veils and curtains and sweeping arcs of
pulsating colored light, you will read my
words and say, "Yes! That's how it was!"

$\mathcal{U}$nder the Big Dipper,
under the North Star's
bright eye
the harvest gleams in our field.
Corn rustles in the rows.
We look up
and the sky begins to move.

Under the Big Dipper,
under the chipped stars
reflected in the lake
we see the ancient tribal gods
begin their ghostly dance.

Above our heads
shimmering curtains
move and part.
The drapery gathers and
falls.
Over the forests of Musquakie land,
the light
begins to flare and twist.
Shining spirits
shake their streaming hair.
We whistle them down the sky.
The dancers bend and leap and run.
Their cloaks unfold and fold
in ruby light.
In dazzling moccasins
they whirl up
and down the dark slopes of air.
The pale fringes of their shawls
hang in ruby light
against the stars.

Nanahbouzho's light
pours over the lake
through pine branches,
through the legends
of the Ottawa.
Light fills our canoe
tied up at the shore.
Light silvers the paddles.

This is midnight,
but behind the hills
the sky is white with beating wings.
We see the same white geese
that live in the old Norse tales—
the trapped white
geese of the northern sky
beating their glistening wings
against those freezing
nets of light.

The sky is moving.
It is rising and falling
where our heavy horses
dream in the meadow.

This is the ancient Nordic blood light
wavering overhead. Torches flare.
Warrior riders send up
their arrows of fire.

Who will claim the flaming
throne
blazing in the blue-black
air
over endless Russian steppes?

The breath of ghostly
Hungarian horses
comes sifting through the dark
like snowy dust, like fiery snow.
Our horses waken. They stand together
with frosty breath.

The silver fire spreads. It curls
high above the rooftop
in the deepest dark
where the sky-fox
swings its snowy tail.
High above the silo and the barn
the sky-fox runs in and
out of the river of light.
Its fur glitters,
lighting the way
for the Lapland herders
keeping watch in the forests below.

Asleep in our quiet beds,
we know of seal lamps
glowing
through frosty igloo walls.
In our dreams we are Inuit.
We call out in our dreams,
"Kick the ball of light,
Ancestors of Ancestors! Kick
the whirling walrus head.
Tumble it back and forth
across the crackling plains
of the blazing sky!"

High above the silo and the barn,
above the dog asleep on the step,
the night sky fills with
rocking light.
Fisherfolk on the cold North Sea
sing of icebergs that tilt
and dip in the salty wind—
good omen of heavy seas to come,
of nets filling with fish.

Luminous in the dark sky-water,
great whales
blow fountains of light.
Their spray powders the horizon.
The sky fills with tinsel—
shakes with the rush and
flow of herring scales.

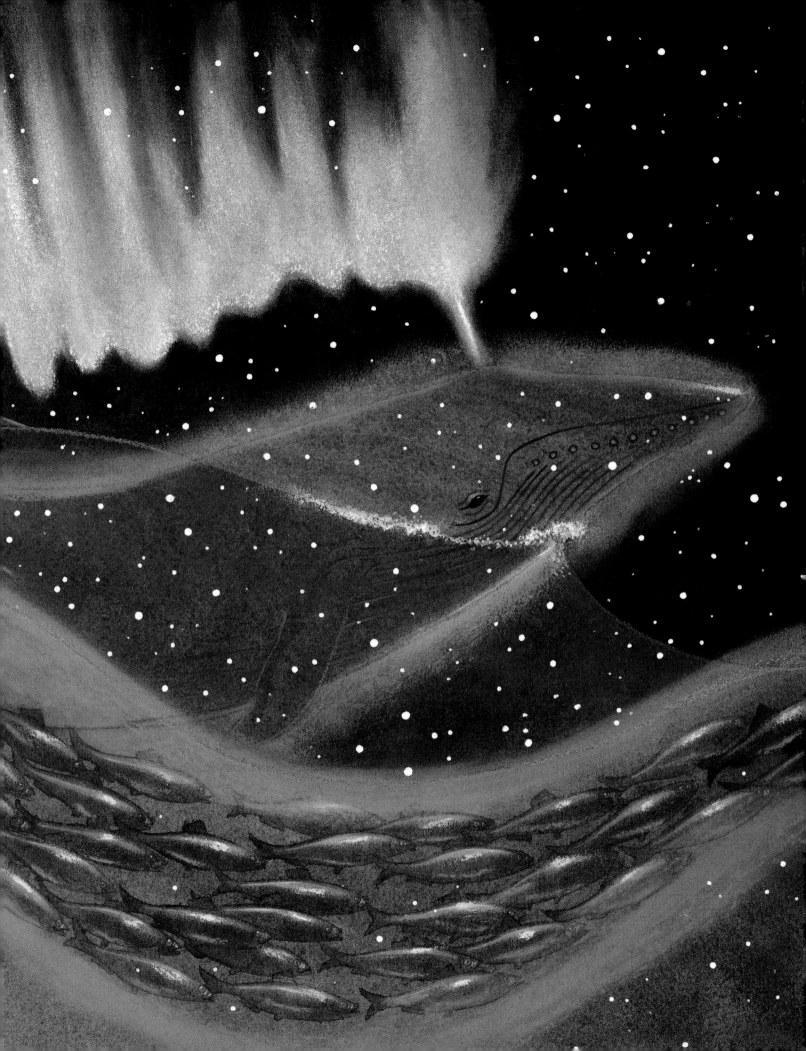

We know these stories.
We watch the skies and we
whisper the words again.

Our dog still sleeps
on the step. The air crackles.
His fur stands up in points.
Sparks hide in his fur.
The sky brightens and
brightens. This is midnight,
but under the Big Dipper,
under our northern sky,
the rooster feels the light
and crows.

LEGENDS ABOUT THE NORTHERN LIGHTS

*F*ROM earliest time, people in northern parts of the world have been amazed, awed, and sometimes frightened by the northern lights. In these spectacular, fiery illuminations, they imagined all sorts of animals, ghosts, dancers, and raging battles.

The Musquakie tribes of North America (also known as the Fox) thought that by whistling they could summon down to earth the leaping, dancing spirits of their ancestors. The Ottawa of Canada told of Nanahbouzho, who created the earth and everything on it. When he went back to his home in the sky, he promised to look after his people. He said he would set flares in the night sky to tell his people that he was always thinking about them and protecting them.

In the far north, the Scandinavians created many tales about the aurora. They told of white geese whose feet had been caught in a sudden freezing of the ice at the North Pole. The northern lights, they said, were the reflections of those wildly beating white wings as the geese tried to free themselves. A Finnish tradition tells of a fox with glittering fur who runs back and forth across the high mountains of Lapland. The old people of Finland still call the northern lights *revontulet*, which means "fox fires."

Many legends tell of raging battles. The Russian poet Mikhail Lomonosov described a battle over a flaming throne in his poem "Ode to the Northern Lights." The Scots, the Hungarians, the Tlingit tribes along the coast of Alaska, and the ancient Norse people all saw the wild movement and red color that sometimes spreads across the sky. Each of these cultures associated this red light with violent battles, perhaps even a prediction of battles yet to come. In some Nordic countries, the word for the northern lights is *blodlyse,* which means "blood light."

Like the Musquakie tribes, other peoples practiced the tradition of whistling at the northern lights. But instead of happily calling down the spirits, the Norwegians feared what might happen if anyone whistled at the lights. They said it was disrespectful and dangerous to try. And if anyone dared to laugh at the lights, it might mean paralysis for the unfortunate person! In Sweden, parents prohibited their children from having their hair cut during an aurora display or going outside without a hat. They feared that the lights would come down and scorch the children's heads.

In parts of Norway, the displays of flickering light were thought to be reflections of huge schools of fish. Old Finnish myths tell of giant whales thrashing the water with their flukes. The people there pictured far-off icebergs rocking in windy seas. The northern lights symbolized good omens for the fishing boats that counted on these catches.

There are many Inuit legends about the aurora borealis. The one in this book tells of a game in the sky played by spirits who use a glowing walrus head. The players must kick the lighted head so that it lands on its tusks.

THE AURORA'S FORMS

QUIET ARCS These arcs—sometimes broad, sometimes narrow—curve like a rainbow. The upper edge is usually fuzzy, and the lower edge is usually sharp. A dark band may appear to be in between. These arcs are generally greenish yellow, sometimes white.

PULSATING ARCS These often appear alone in the sky and are usually bluish green. Part or all of the arc flashes upward in a pulsating movement at regular intervals of a few seconds.

BANDS Bands are not as regular as arcs and may curve like a semicircle. Bands are never still but move about rapidly.

CURTAINS In this variation of a band aurora, the bands are crossed vertically by dark, shadowy areas, so that they look like vast, heavy curtains hanging down from somewhere high up in the sky. They are usually bluish-greenish white and move as though being slowly blown by a breeze.

RAYS These look like giant searchlights shining up into the sky. They can appear alone or in bundles, and sometimes seem to be pulled into the shape of a fan.

CORONA This display is composed of rays or bands that seem to converge at one single point in the sky.

LUMINOUS AND PULSATING SURFACES These usually appear after an intense display of curtains or rays and look like colored clouds. The cloudlike shapes may pulsate, appearing and disappearing rhythmically. They can be pale violet, rose, or red.

FLAMING AURORAS These arc-shaped waves of light move quickly upward, one after another, like flames.

A NOTE ABOUT THE AURORA

IN HIS diary entry for September 24, 1732, the famous scientist Anders Celsius made a note about the northern lights. Even though we honor him for giving us the Celsius thermometer scale, he mistakenly thought the northern lights were caused by volcanoes erupting near the North Pole!

Modern science tells us that the story starts at the sun, where electrically charged particles are sent streaming into space. This rushing stream is called the solar wind, and it is constantly moving toward the earth at incredible speeds.

Sometimes there is an explosive release of energy from the sun, a solar flare. These solar flares cause magnetic storms and intense gusts of solar wind. As the electrically charged particles approach the earth, they are guided by the earth's magnetic field toward our North and South Poles.

When these charged particles hit the earth's upper atmosphere, they cause the atoms and molecules of oxygen and nitrogen to glow with the flaring rivers and curtains of color and light that we call the aurora borealis or the northern lights. People who live in the farthest southern latitudes can see explosions of light coming from the south magnetic pole. These are known as the aurora australis. Astronauts high above the earth have seen the aurora borealis as a circle of flaring light crowning the North Pole.

The colors in the aurora come from the light given off when the particles in the solar wind hit the gases in the earth's atmosphere. Most of the color comes from oxygen; some of it is the result of charged particles colliding with nitrogen. The light is usually white, green, or red. These colors combine into other colors too. Less often, the aurora can glow a hard-to-see orange-red or a violet and blue visible only in moonlight.

No aurora comes closer to the earth than forty miles. The display can reach several hundred miles above our planet.

The aurora is *always* present. Charged particles from the sun enter our atmosphere at all times. However, the aurora goes unseen in the daytime because of sunlight, and at night it can be too faint to be noticed.

For my son, Kai, who brought me to the old farm road one cold
midnight to see the aurora flaring against the dark sky,
with love—B.J.E.

For Barbara, whose radiant enthusiasm rivaled the aurora.
And for Tory—thank you for your confidence in me.
—H.K.D.

Interested readers can consult three good sources for more information:
Asgeir Brekke and Alv Egeland, *The Northern Light: From Mythology to Space
Research* (Berlin, New York: Springer Verlag, 1983); Neil Davis, *The Aurora
Watcher's Handbook* (Fairbanks: University of Alaska Press, 1992); and
Candace Savage, *Aurora: The Mysterious Northern Lights*
(San Francisco: Sierra Club Books, 1994).

Call (303) 497-3235 to find out when to watch for the aurora. Listen to the
taped message, and if the "Boulder K index" is five or above and the sky is
clear, head for an open field.

Orchard Books, A Grolier Company, 95 Madison Avenue, New York, NY 10016

Manufactured in the United States of America. Printed and bound by Phoenix Color Corp.
The text of this book is set in 18 point Bembo Bold. The illustrations are pastel and gouache.
1 3 5 7 9 10 8 6 4 2

Library of Congress Cataloging-in-Publication Data
Esbensen, Barbara Juster.
The night rainbow / by Barbara Juster Esbensen ; illustrated by Helen K. Davie. p. cm.
Summary: A poem based on ancient legends about the northern lights from people who associated
the fiery illuminations with animals, ghosts, dancers, and raging battles.
ISBN 0-531-30244-X (trade : alk. paper).—ISBN 0-531-33244-6 (lib. bdg. : alk. paper)
1. Indian astronomy—North America—Juvenile literature. 2. Auroras—North America Juvenile
literature. 3. Indians of North America—Folklore. [1. Auroras Folklore Poetry.
2. Folklore Poetry. 3. American Poetry.] I. Davie, Helen, ill. II. Title.
E98.A88E72 2000
538'.768—dc21 99-30880